THE PLAIN-ENGLISH GUIDE TO DEVELOPING AN ECONOMIC SANCTIONS PROGRAM

Second Edition

By Heidi Hunter

LitAbby Press

St. Paul, Minnesota

The Plain-English Guide to Developing an Economic Sanctions Program
Second Edition

First Printing: June 2024
Second Printing: July 2025

Published by LilAbby Press
St. Paul, Minnesota
Printed in the United States of America

ISBN: 979-8-9994289-0-5 (paperback)
979-8-9994289-1-2 (ebook)

cover design by Heidi Hunter

TABLE OF CONTENTS

DISCLAIMER 1
INTRODUCTION 2
DEFINITIONS 4
1 BRIEF REFRESHER ON ECONOMIC SANCTIONS 10
2 SANCTIONS PROGRAM 14
3 SANCTIONS COMPLIANCE OFFICER/RESPONSIBLE PARTY 15
4 ECONOMIC SANCTIONS POLICY 18
5 RISK ASSESSMENT 23
6 INTERNAL CONTROLS 36
7 DUE DILIGENCE 39
8 SETTING UP A SCANNING PROGRAM 42
9 WRITTEN SANCTIONS PROCEDURES 53
10 SANCTIONS CLAUSES 56
11 ENVIRONMENTAL SCANNING 61
12 TRAINING 64
13 AUDITING/TESTING 69
14 DOCUMENTATION 72
15 PENALTIES FOR NON-COMPLIANCE 73
16 CONCLUSION 75
REFERENCES 76
AUTHOR BIOGRAPHY 77
ALL BOOKS IN THE PLAIN-ENGLISH GUIDE SERIES BY HEIDI HUNTER 78
NOTES 79

Disclaimer

The information provided in this book is for informational purposes only and is not intended to constitute legal advice. The author of this book is not an attorney, is not providing legal advice, and is not creating an attorney-client relationship with the reader.

Readers should not act or rely on any information in this book without seeking the advice of a lawyer. Any reliance upon the information contained in this guide is solely at the reader's own risk.

The author makes no representations or warranties about the completeness, accuracy, reliability, or suitability of the information in this book.

While every effort has been made to provide accurate and complete guidance, it's important to understand that this guide does not guarantee an effective sanctions compliance program free from fines or penalties. Compliance with economic sanctions regulations is a complex and evolving area, and the effectiveness of any program depends on various factors, including the specific circumstances of your business and the actions of relevant regulatory authorities. Therefore, the author cannot guarantee specific outcomes or results from implementing the suggestions provided in this guide. It's essential to use this information as a tool to develop and enhance your sanctions compliance program, but the ultimate responsibility for compliance rests with the reader and their organization.

In no event shall the author be liable for any loss or damage whatsoever arising from, or in connection with, the use of the information contained in this book.

Introduction

Economic sanctions are powerful tools governments and international bodies use to influence the behavior of nations, organizations, and individuals. Navigating the complex sanctions landscape can be challenging for businesses, big or small, domestic or international.

That's why I created *The Plain-English Guide to Economic Sanctions* series of books, to help fellow colleagues navigate complex sanctions issues with confidence.

Welcome to the second, updated edition of *The Plain-English Guide to Developing an Economic Sanctions Program.* This book aims to help readers understand the key parts of an effective sanctions compliance program and how to implement them. It's useful for anyone who needs to create a program for their business or strengthen their company's program.

If you're new to sanctions or need a refresher, the first book in this series, *The Plain-English Guide to Economic Sanctions*, provides a comprehensive overview. This guide assumes you are at least familiar with the concepts and terms in that guide.

This guide focuses on setting up a program to comply with economic sanctions overseen by the Office of Foreign Assets Control (OFAC). Trade sanctions administered by other government agencies, such as the Department of State or the Bureau of Industry and Security, won't be covered in detail. Complying with the sanctions regimes of foreign governments is also outside the scope of this book.

Sanctions compliance isn't just about avoiding fines. It is about upholding ethical and legal standards while navigating a complex global landscape. However, violations can result in substantial fines, and civil and criminal penalties can exceed several million dollars,[1] leading to negative publicity about your company and damaging your reputation with customers and business partners.

OFAC has overseen many public enforcement actions and assessed numerous civil monetary penalties where deficiencies in a company's sanctions compliance program were identified as a cause of the sanctions violations.[2]

Even with a robust compliance program, you might still face fines for accidental violations. However, OFAC considers a strong compliance program a positive factor when determining penalties. On the other hand, the lack of a sanctions compliance program is often seen as an aggravating factor that can lead to higher fines.[3]

The tips in this guide draw on the author's experience, industry practices, and OFAC compliance guidance. You may also find the companion workbook, *The Plain-English Guide to Developing an Economic Sanctions Program Workbook*, helpful as you build or update your own program.

Definitions

Some of the terms referenced in this guide are defined below.

Beneficial Owner

The person who ultimately owns, benefits from, or controls an asset.

Blocking Program

An OFAC sanctions program that requires a sanctioned party's assets to be blocked or frozen. US persons are prohibited from doing business with them.

Bureau of Industry and Security (BIS)

The US Department of Commerce's Bureau of Industry and Security (BIS) administers and enforces export controls on dual-use and certain munitions items.

Business Partner/Third Party

Any external third party you do business with. A business partner can be a vendor, a subcontractor, an attorney, a joint venture partner, a consultant, a distributor or wholesaler, a supplier, or an agent or representative acting on a company's behalf.

Comprehensive Sanctions

A trade embargo against a country. Most transactions are prohibited. Countries under comprehensive sanctions are Iran, Cuba, Syria[4], North Korea, and Russian-held areas of Ukraine, such as Crimea.

Control Gap

An internal control either does not exist or does not function properly.

Debt/Equity Restrictions

OFAC restricts the issuance of long-term debt (with terms over fourteen or thirty days, for example) or the purchase of equity for some non-SDN parties. "Debt" includes bonds, loans, extensions of credit, loan guarantees, letters of credit, discount notes or bills, or commercial paper, while equity includes stocks and shares.[5]

Department of State (DoS)

The Department of State has several divisions that oversee the export of defense-related items and services and weapons of mass destruction.

Dual-Use Goods

Goods, software, and technology that can be used for both civilian and military purposes.

Economic Sanctions

The government's restrictions or penalties on individuals, entities, groups, governments, or countries to achieve particular foreign policy or national security goals.

Environmental Scanning

Also known as e-scanning. Environmental scanning is how you, as the sanctions compliance professional, stay updated on changes in economic sanctions regulations.

Executive Order

When the President wants to impose new economic sanctions, he will issue an Executive Order. The Executive Order explains why sanctions are needed, the laws under which the Executive Order is created, and who can be sanctioned under the program.

Facilitation

Assisting others in conducting a transaction that violates sanctions if you had conducted it yourself.

Freezing or Blocking Assets

Preventing a sanctioned party from accessing or using assets you hold that belong to them, such as a bank account or an insurance policy. Assets are deposited into a blocked bank account when possible.

Fuzzy Logic

A sanctions screening application that employs fuzzy logic uses variations in spelling, phonetics, and name transposition (switching of first and last names, for example) to determine a possible match.

Indirect

Selling goods or services to someone acting on behalf of a sanctioned party or country.

Internal Controls

Internal controls are the processes, procedures, and measures that prevent and detect sanctions violations.

List-Based Sanctions

Programs where sanctioned parties are added to the Specially Designated Nationals (SDN) list. Most transactions with them are prohibited, and assets you hold that belong to them may need to be blocked.

Nexus

Transactions connected to the US, such as participation by a US party, sale of a US good or service, and transacting in US dollars or through the US financial system. Non-US persons carrying out a transaction outside the US may be required to comply with US sanctions if that transaction has a US nexus.

The term is also used when referencing whether a particular transaction, claim, or policy has a connection to a sanctioned country, party, or good.

Office of Foreign Assets Control (OFAC)

The Office of Foreign Assets Control (OFAC), part of the US Department of the Treasury, oversees most US sanctions programs.

OFAC Regulations

OFAC incorporates sanctions laws and executive orders into its own regulations for a program, which are issued in the Code of Federal

Regulations (CFR). The CFR is where all rules implemented by the Federal government are published.

OFAC Sanctions

Sanctions administered by the Office of Foreign Assets Control (OFAC). You'll see terms like "economic sanctions," "OFAC sanctions," "trade sanctions," "sanctions regulations," "OFAC regulations," and "US sanctions" used interchangeably in this guide.

Possible Match/False Positive/Positive Match

A possible match occurs when your sanctions screening system identifies a customer who may be a match to a person on the SDN list. A possible or potential match is also known as an "alert" or a "hit." "Possible match," "potential match," "alert," and "hit" are used interchangeably within this guide.

A false positive is a hit, which, after reviewing additional information on the customer and sanctioned party, is not an actual match. A positive match, on the other hand, is an alert that is determined to be an actual match once your customer's information is compared to the sanctioned party's information.

Risk Assessment

A risk assessment is a method for identifying, analyzing, and addressing a company's sanctions risks. It helps pinpoint any weaknesses in the program and lays out a plan to fix them.

Root Cause

The root cause is the main reason why a process failed.

Secondary Sanctions

Also known as "extraterritorial sanctions." Under certain programs, like those related to Iran or Russia, non-US persons may face penalties under US law for prohibited activities, even if they have no ties, connections, or nexus to the US. Additionally, US entities will be prohibited from engaging in transactions with these penalized parties.

Specially Designated National (SDN)/Sanctioned Party

An individual, company, organization, group, government, vessel, or aircraft sanctioned by OFAC and listed on the Specially Designated Nationals (SDN) list. Their assets are blocked, and US persons are generally prohibited from dealing with them.[6]

Sanctions Compliance Officer (SCO)

The person within an organization with ultimate responsibility for the sanctions compliance program.

Sanctions Compliance Program (SCP)

A sanctions compliance program (SCP) encompasses the policies, procedures, and controls that enable a company to comply with sanctions regulations.

Sanctions Compliance/Sanctions Compliance Team

Sanctions compliance is the function within a company responsible for managing the policy, program, and controls related to sanctions compliance. The SCO is part of this function. This function may also include a separate team dedicated to sanctions (i.e., the Sanctions Compliance Team).

Sanctions Evasion

Sanctions evasion occurs when parties attempt to structure a transaction to get around sanctions.

Sanctions Program

A sanctions program consists of all the laws, Executive Orders, OFAC regulations, guidance, licenses, and FAQs related to restrictions against a specific country or activity. It governs what you can and cannot do.

Sanctions Risk

Sanctions risk refers to potential threats or weaknesses that, if not properly managed by internal controls, can result in violations of OFAC's regulations.

Scanning/Screening

Reviewing a customer or transaction to identify potential sanctions issues. This can involve scanning a customer or payee name against OFAC's watchlists or reviewing a transaction for a sanctions nexus.

The 50 Percent Rule

Entities that are majority-owned (50 percent or more) by one or more blocked persons, either through direct or indirect ownership, are also considered sanctioned, despite not being named on a sanctions list.

Threshold

A threshold is the level at which the sanctions screening application considers a party a potential match to a sanctioned party. One hundred percent generally means an exact name match. Lower thresholds (such as 95 percent) mean it is a possible match based on fuzzy logic. For example, your customer "Jose C. Rodriguez" may match against "Jose Rodrigues" or "Jose P Rodriguez" at a 95 percent threshold.

US Person

US citizens anywhere in the world, US-incorporated businesses, including their foreign branches, people who are in the US for any reason, even if they are citizens of another country, and any persons transacting in the US financial system, US dollars, or US goods.

Watchlists

Watchlists are lists maintained by OFAC of individuals and entities designated as sanctioned parties. These lists can be Specially Designated Nationals (SDN) lists and non-SDN lists. These lists specify various prohibitions, from full asset and transaction bans (for those on the SDN lists) to targeted restrictions (for those on the non-SDN lists).

1
Brief Refresher on Economic Sanctions

Sanctions are restrictions or penalties that governments impose on countries, individuals, groups, governments, or industries to help achieve specific foreign policy and national security objectives. For example, the United States may prohibit US citizens from engaging in particular trade or financial activities, or other dealings, unless they get permission from OFAC or are expressly allowed to by law.[7] Since each sanctions program is based on different foreign policy and national security goals, prohibitions can vary from one program to another.[8]

At its simplest, economic sanctions mean you are not allowed to do business with certain countries or parties. Before proceeding with a business transaction, you must do your homework to identify any potential sanctions issues.

Many countries have their own sanctions laws. If your company conducts business in multiple countries, such as selling to foreign customers, trading internationally, or working with foreign business partners, you may need to comply with sanctions rules from several countries.

The Office of Foreign Assets Control (OFAC), part of the US Department of the Treasury, oversees most US sanctions programs. Some trade sanctions are managed by different agencies, including the Department of State (DoS) and the Bureau of Industry and Security (BIS) within the Department of Commerce. These export control restrictions work in conjunction with OFAC sanctions.

Most sanctions programs are established and administered through Executive Orders issued by the President, laws established by Congress, and regulations established by OFAC.

OFAC administers sanctions programs that consist of all the laws, Executive Orders, OFAC regulations, guidance, licenses, and FAQs related to restrictions against a specific country or activity. Some programs target activities in certain countries, such as Cuba, while some target specific activities globally, such as narcotics trafficking and weapons proliferation.

A country-based program does not mean that only people in that country are sanctioned. Parties anywhere in the world can be sanctioned under any program, including persons in the US and those in your country. For example, the Russian Harmful Foreign Activities Program imposes sanctions against individuals and entities anywhere in the world involved in specified harmful foreign activities of the Russian Federation.[9]

Also, programs may not exist indefinitely. For example, Sudan used to have a trade embargo, but it was discontinued several years ago, and Sudan is currently subject to only minimal sanctions.

The best place to find all of these documents is on the specific program's page on the OFAC website, the link for which is provided under References.

OFAC's definition of a US person is broad and can extend to individuals and businesses outside the US in certain situations.

You are required to comply with US sanctions if one of the following conditions exist:

- You are covered under the definition of a US Person.
- You are conducting a transaction with a US nexus.
- You are conducting activity covered by OFAC's secondary sanctions.

You are a US Person and are covered by US sanctions in the following situations:

- US citizens anywhere in the world
- US-incorporated businesses, including their foreign branches
- people in the US for any reason, even if they are citizens of another country
- any party using the US financial system, US dollars, or US goods[10]

This means a foreign bank without US branches must also follow OFAC rules if it uses US dollars or the US financial system for a transaction.

There are situations where foreign parties may need to comply with US sanctions:

- US-nexus transactions
- secondary sanctions
- foreign subsidiaries of US entities for certain programs, namely Cuba, Iran, and North Korea

The term "sanctions" covers a wide range of actions the United States can take against a country, government, person, group, or industry, depending on what activity the US wants to stop. Generally, sanctions fall into three main categories: list-based sanctions, comprehensive country sanctions, and sectoral or trade sanctions.[11]

The most challenging part of complying with sanctions is when parties are considered sanctioned despite not appearing on any SDN or Non-SDN list. This can occur in a couple of ways.

First, some OFAC sanctions block categories of persons even if they do not appear on the SDN List.[12] For example, for the Venezuelan sanctions program, Executive Order 13884 blocks any person who meets the definition of the "Government of Venezuela."[13] Also, OFAC's Cuba sanctions prohibit most transactions with Cuban nationals.[14]

The second way is commonly referred to as the "50 Percent Rule."[15] This rule applies when a company is majority-owned (i.e., 50 percent or more) by one or more sanctioned parties. This includes both direct and indirect ownership. These entities are considered sanctioned even if they aren't on the SDN list.

No official government list of companies owned by sanctioned parties exists; however, some private companies, such as Dow Jones, create and maintain such lists.

Economic sanctions impact your entire organization—every employee, every department, and every business line—especially in global industries. The need to be knowledgeable about and comply with sanctions does not end with compliance professionals. Employees handling tasks with a sanctions nexus must also understand and adhere to sanctions requirements.

This list isn't exhaustive, but it highlights key roles that may have a sanctions nexus that will need sanctions procedures and training within your organization:

- payment processors (such as a payment for goods or services, claim, refund, or vendor payment)
- originate a payment on an account
- open new accounts
- underwrite policies or loans
- conduct customer due diligence
- import or export goods
- conduct marine shipments

- contract with vendors or other business partners
- sell products or services
- hire staff
- claims adjustors
- product development
- legal/compliance
- customer service

Now that you have a solid refresher on how sanctions work, it's time to focus on preventing violations within your company. The next section kicks off with the most crucial step: building a robust economic sanctions compliance program.

These topics are explored in more detail in *The Plain-English Guide to Economic Sanctions,* the first book in the series.

2
Sanctions Program

How Do I Comply with Economic Sanctions?

OFAC prohibits all parties subject to US sanctions from doing business with sanctioned parties. How you follow that requirement is up to you.

Begin by setting up a basic sanctions compliance program that outlines how you will comply with regulations. If you already have a program, compare it to OFAC's recommendations to identify necessary improvements.[16]

Establish a Sanctions Program

A sanctions compliance program (SCP) comprises the policies, procedures, and controls that enable a company to follow sanctions regulations. Depending on your company's size and whether it operates worldwide or solely within the United States, your program might include some or all of these elements. In subsequent chapters, we'll go into more detail about each component.

- a Sanctions Compliance Officer (SCO) or other responsible party–Chapter 3
- an economic sanctions policy–Chapter 4
- a risk assessment–Chapter 5
- internal controls–Chapters 6
- customer and vendor due diligence–Chapter 7
- sanctions screening program–Chapter 8
- written procedures–Chapter 9
- contract language–Chapter 10
- environmental scanning–Chapter 10
- training–Chapter 11
- auditing and testing–Chapter 12

The Plain-English Guide to Developing an Economic Sanctions Program Workbook can help you develop your program with easy-to-use worksheets that cover every step in the process.

Let's discuss these key sections of an SCP in more detail.

3

Sanctions Compliance Officer/Responsible Party

Someone within the company should be responsible for overseeing the SCP. This includes oversight for all aspects of the program, direct supervision of the sanctions compliance team if there is one, and indirect oversight of any additional staff performing sanctions-related duties.

In larger companies, the person may be referred to as the sanctions compliance officer (SCO). OFAC does not require a company to appoint an SCO, but it recommends it in its compliance guidance.[17] In larger companies, it is a good idea for someone to hold this title so that employees know who to contact with questions about sanctions. Alternatively, these duties may rest with the chief compliance officer (CCO), chief risk officer (CRO), or chief legal officer (CLO), who may have other responsibilities in addition to sanctions compliance.

The SCO should have enough independence and authority to act within the company. Ideally, this should be someone at the management level or higher. The person should be allowed to take necessary actions to address any issues with the sanctions program. They should have direct access to senior management without having to go through multiple management layers. Periodic meetings with senior management should take place to update them on the status of the sanctions program.

The sanctions function overseen by the SCO may be a stand-alone group (referred to as the "sanctions compliance team" or just "sanctions compliance") or part of a larger group, such as financial crimes or the anti-money laundering team. The sanctions function may also include staff in other departments whose jobs have a sanctions nexus (such as accounts payable).

Some responsibilities of the sanctions compliance officer include:

- maintaining and updating the economic sanctions policy
- developing procedures
- conducting the risk assessment
- overseeing staff who perform sanctions-related procedures
- administering sanctions training

- working with other teams within the company to implement sanctions controls
- updating senior management on sanctions issues and projects
- acting as a liaison with external legal counsel
- filing required reports with OFAC

The SCO should also have enough resources to do their job effectively. This includes having the correct number of staff with the necessary expertise and access to technology, training, and other resources needed to adequately manage sanctions compliance.

Risk Decision Matrix

Bigger companies, however, might not want the Sanctions Compliance Officer (SCO) to make all the sanctions-related decisions alone. In these cases, a risk decision matrix can be helpful. It clearly shows who in the company is responsible for making certain sanctions decisions. At my previous job, we often used one when facing tough sanctions discussions. Our matrix was a simple Excel sheet with five levels of decision-making based on the situation.

Tier 1: Business line staff make the decisions. No sanctions issue exists, so the employees conduct business as usual.

Tier 2: The sanctions compliance team makes the decision. Someone on the sanctions team can resolve a potential sanctions issue, such as clearing a false positive match.

Tier 3: The SCO or the sanctions compliance team manager makes the decision. Potential business that may violate sanctions is escalated to the manager or the SCO. They can decline the business if a transaction or account violates OFAC sanctions. Otherwise, if necessary, they can resolve the issue with input from other company staff.

Tier 4: Business line management makes the decision. Usually, these decisions are risk-related. A sanctions issue affects a line of business. The customer or transaction is a high risk for a potential sanctions violation, so the decision is whether you accept the customer or conduct the transaction. Business line management has the final say, although the SCO and legal counsel may provide input during the decision-making process. This tier is not for transactions that clearly violate sanctions; such decisions rest with the sanctions compliance staff in Tier 3.

Tier 5: Senior management is involved in the decision-making process. A sanctions violation may have occurred, so executive management is involved in determining the response with input from the SCO, legal counsel, and business line staff.

4
Economic Sanctions Policy

The cornerstone of the SCP is an economic sanctions policy, which outlines your company's commitment to sanctions compliance and provides a brief description of the procedures and controls in place for compliance.

Key best practices when drafting or updating your sanctions policy:

- It should be risk-based and tailored to your company's specific risks.
- It should be written in plain, easy-to-read language since everyone in the company must be familiar with it.
- If employees are located in foreign countries, it should be translated into their native language.
- It should be reviewed and updated annually or whenever significant updates are made to sanctions regulations or your program.
- It should be stored in an area (such as an online shared site) where all staff can review it.

Your policy should include high-level information on the following key components:

- senior management's commitment to fostering a culture of compliance
- sanctions laws applicable to your company, both domestic and foreign
- pertinent definitions for key terms such as sanctions, sanctioned parties, prohibited transactions, etc.
- potential penalties to the company and the individual for non-compliance
- who the policy applies to in the company, and whether third parties such as vendors and business partners must comply with your policy
- the person responsible for the program and their duties
- that a risk assessment is conducted
- high-level description of internal controls
- who will receive sanctions training
- testing and auditing of the program
- methods to report potential violations

These sections are discussed in more detail below.

Senior Management Commitment

OFAC believes senior management's commitment and support for an organization's SCP are crucial factors in determining its success.[18] Senior management's commitment also demonstrates to the rest of the company that sanctions compliance is a priority for the firm's success.

Your policy should clearly state that senior management is committed to sanctions compliance and will not conduct business that violates sanctions.

Unfortunately, there have been many cases where companies, despite having what appeared to be robust sanctions compliance programs, received hefty fines from OFAC. This occurs when senior management merely pays lip service to compliance and undermines controls to carry out transactions that breach sanctions or aid sanctioned parties and countries.

Some considerations that will demonstrate senior management's commitment to OFAC:[19]

- Sanctions compliance should be part of an overall "culture of compliance" within your company. This means your company and its senior management are dedicated to ethics and compliance in all aspects of its business dealings, not just sanctions. If your company has a Code of Ethics, sanctions should be included.
- Senior management should review and approve the SCP.
- The sanctions compliance function should receive adequate resources, such as the appropriate number of staff with sufficient expertise, technology, training, and other resources to support compliance.
- The sanctions compliance function should have sufficient authority and autonomy within the company. This means the person appointed to oversee sanctions compliance should be at a level within the company that allows them to work independently and take any appropriate actions to address issues with the sanctions program.
- Senior management should be involved when potential regulatory violations occur or when material deficiencies are identified in the program. They should also approve how gaps or issues are corrected and any OFAC filings.

Pertinent Definitions for Key Terms

Since your policy will need to be read and understood by all employees, even those who don't regularly work in positions that encounter sanctions issues, you should define key terms such as "sanctions," "sanctioned parties or Specially Designated Nationals (SDNs)," and "prohibited transactions" as well as any other technical terms that are in your policy. Reviewing the definitions at the beginning of this guide may be a good starting point.

Sanctions Laws Applicable to Your Company

This section should state what jurisdiction(s) your company is subject to. If you are solely a domestic company with no foreign customers, business partners, vendors, or sales, then you may only be subject to US sanctions (OFAC). If you conduct business globally, you may want to mention other jurisdictions in which you regularly operate, such as Canada, the United Kingdom (UK), or the European Union (EU), as your company will need to comply with sanctions in those jurisdictions as well.

Potential Penalties for Non-Compliance

This section should briefly explain the penalties for sanctions violations to the company and the individual employee. The penalties should include potential monetary fines, job-related consequences such as termination, jail time, and negative media coverage against the company.

Who the Policy Applies to

This paragraph should explain that the policy applies to everyone within the company, from line staff up to executives and the Board of Directors. You may also want it to apply to external parties, such as business partners, joint venture partners, vendors, contractors, etc. If you do, you will want to ensure that these third parties are aware of your policy and its expectations. My prior company had a Vendor Code of Ethics that outlined our expectations for ethical behavior, including compliance with sanctions. Our vendors had to follow these policies.

Responsibilities

Your policy should clearly state that the SCO is responsible for the sanctions compliance program and might also list some of the key responsibilities.

Risk Assessment

This section will mention that your sanctions compliance program is based on risk and may briefly describe how risk is determined. A separate written procedure or an addendum to the policy may describe in detail how the risk assessment should be conducted. Completing a risk assessment will be discussed in more detail in a later section, as well as in *The Plain-English Guide to Economic Sanctions Risk Assessments*.

Internal Controls

Internal controls are the processes, procedures, and measures that prevent and detect sanctions violations. Your policy may list high-level controls such as sanctions screening and exclusion language in contracts.

Training

Everyone in an organization likely needs basic sanctions knowledge and training. Some employees who regularly encounter sanctions issues may require more detailed training. You should describe in your sanctions policy the company's commitment to ensuring all employees receive sanctions training, who will receive sanctions training, how often it will be rolled out, how it will be tracked, and who will provide it.

Testing and Auditing

Your sanctions program should be reviewed and tested to identify any gaps that may prevent it from operating effectively. This can be done through periodic compliance testing and auditing.

The policy should specify that testing and auditing will occur, who will conduct it, and the frequency. It's okay to specify the frequency as "periodically" or "at least once every three years."

Reporting Violations

Depending on your company's size, employees may have multiple ways to report inappropriate conduct. Some examples may include contacting a manager, calling an anonymous hotline, or escalating to the SCO or the CCO.

If you find drafting a policy daunting, many companies post their sanctions compliance policy online. You can find plenty of examples to get you started writing your own policy.

5
Risk Assessment

OFAC recommends that organizations take a risk-based approach to their sanctions compliance program (SCP). But what does that mean? To develop an effective SCP, you must evaluate and understand your company's specific sanctions exposures. This requires conducting a thorough assessment of your risk factors.

What Is Risk?

According to OFAC, sanctions risks are potential threats or vulnerabilities that, if ignored or not properly handled, can lead to violations of OFAC's regulations and negatively affect an organization's reputation and business.[20]

In other words, considering your company's unique situation, how likely is it that your company may violate sanctions regulations when conducting business?

What Is a Risk Assessment and Why Is It Important?

A sanctions risk assessment (SRA) is a method for identifying, analyzing, and addressing a company's sanctions risks. It helps pinpoint any weaknesses in the program and lays out a plan to fix them. The primary goal of an SRA is to evaluate and reduce the risk of sanctions violations, ensuring compliance with OFAC regulations. By identifying gaps and strengthening controls, an SRA ensures compliance with OFAC regulations, minimizes financial penalties for violations, and protects an entity's reputation in the marketplace.

What Criteria Should Be Assessed?

As recommended by OFAC, you can start by identifying risks associated with your **customers, products, services, and locations**. However, there are several other risk categories you should also include, depending on your type of business:

- supply chains
- distribution channels
- counterparties/third-party associates

- types of transactions
- governmental contracts
- technology

For larger entities, you may want to assess these items at the corporate level and separately by business unit or location. For example, at my previous company, we separately evaluated the risk categories for our foreign entities and distinct business units of our domestic entities, such as group benefits insurance, personal insurance, commercial insurance, and treasury. I then rolled those up into a corporate-level assessment.

At the most basic level, you want to identify which of your customers, products, services, and locations pose the highest risk of a sanctions violation.

Assessing the Criteria

Below are examples of questions to ask when building your risk assessment, along with guidance on how to analyze the responses. Similar questions and analyses can be conducted for the other risk criteria.

Customers

Who are your customers? Are they individuals, small businesses, or corporations? Do you have a steady base of customers, or are you expanding and bringing in many new customers? What industries do you typically target for customers?

Businesses pose a higher risk than individuals because it's easier to conceal the true ownership of a company. A stable customer base poses less risk, as you know their usual transaction patterns. On the other hand, new clients are riskier because you're not yet familiar with them and the types of transactions they'll carry out.

The type of industry a customer operates in also affects risk. Customers in the military, defense, and technology sectors would be at higher risk for sanctions violations than those in industries such as food and clothing, for example.

Products

What specific products and services do you sell?

Identify the various types of products you sell, as they carry different risk levels. For instance, if you sell financial products, allowing online account opening poses a higher risk than those requiring in-person verification. Similarly, certain goods may entail greater risk depending on their industry use. For example, office chairs typically pose a low risk. In contrast, laptops may pose a higher risk if your customers are military contractors rather than schools.

If you provide a service as your "product," consider whether the service is high-risk or is used by high-risk customers. For example, a business offering payday loans has a higher sanctions risk than a business offering plumbing services.

Services

What services do you offer your customers?

This is distinct from whether your "product" is a service.

Do you provide correspondent banking services, online account setup, Automated Clearing House (ACH), or wire transactions? All of these may pose a higher risk. Additionally, extending credit to your customers can also increase risk.

How services are provided also impacts risk. Online transactions or services handled by third-party providers are riskier than those provided by company employees in person. When you offer services online, it's harder to be sure who you're actually doing business with.

Locations

Where do you have employees? Where do you do business (sell goods, have offices, or provide services)? Do you have any business partners (vendors, etc.) in foreign locations?

Each country carries its own sanctions risk. Businesses in higher-risk jurisdictions (explained more fully later in this chapter) pose a higher risk of sanctions violations to your company.

You will want to identify which countries your products or services are sold in, and a breakdown of the largest jurisdictions. For example, if you decide that China is a high-risk jurisdiction for your company, but only .01 percent of your sales are made there, will you want to focus all of your sanctions controls on that business? Or will you want to focus more on Russia, which is also considered a higher-risk jurisdiction, where 20 percent of your sales are?

You will gather this information through meetings and questionnaires with staff from other business units, as well as a review of internal and external company documents.

Examples

Let's apply these concepts to a couple of examples.

First, a rudimentary assessment for a small business called Barb's Baubles:

> Our customers are primarily individuals, and we have about 50% repeat customers. We sell handmade jewelry products of moderate value ($50-$250 range). Sales are done online rather than in person, and we accept credit cards and payment services, including PayPal and Venmo. We sell anywhere in the world, but primarily in the US, Canada, and the UK. Our jewelry artists are all located in the US.

On the other hand, a rudimentary assessment for a larger company such as ABC Company might be:

> Our customers are primarily businesses, including wholesalers who sell our products to other companies. We sell a variety of computer parts online and in person. These customers are located worldwide. We have manufacturing facilities in China, India, and Canada, as well as sales offices in ten additional countries in Europe and Latin America. Our sales breakdown is as follows: 25 percent of our product is sold within the US, 25 percent in the UK and the EU, 25 percent in Latin America, and 25 percent in the rest of the world, with China being the largest purchaser. We have employees in the US, at our three foreign manufacturing facilities, and in our ten sales offices. We extend credit for sales and accept checks, credit cards, payment services such as PayPal, and cryptocurrency.

You can probably see that while Barb's Baubles may have some sanctions risk, ABC Company has a much higher risk.

How Is Risk Score Determined?

The sanctions risk for each criterion must be assessed and given a risk score. A risk score is a categorical value assigned to a risk based on its assessed impact and likelihood of occurrence. This score helps prioritize which risks need immediate attention and action. The scores of high, medium, and low are used to arrive at the company's overall risk level. I also preferred using medium-high and medium-low settings, which are most useful for larger companies.

Below are general definitions of high, medium, and low risk:

High risk: Indicates the significant possibility of a sanctions violation occurring in the current state. Includes a substantial potential for severe consequences. These risks require urgent attention and robust controls to mitigate them.

Medium risk: Denotes a moderate possibility of a sanctions violation occurring in the current state with a modest potential for financial or reputational impact. These risks need regular monitoring and adequate controls, but are less urgent than high-risk ones.

Low risk: Suggests a low likelihood of occurrence in the current state, with a minimal potential financial or reputational impact. These risks require routine checks but generally do not need immediate or intensive controls.[21]

So, the question on your mind is likely: How do I determine whether something is high, medium, or low risk? This will vary from entity to entity and is somewhat subjective based on the assessor's knowledge of sanctions and familiarity with the company and its industry. It can depend on factors such as the financial impact, whether there would be publicity, whether your company operates globally, and whether the industries it operates in are frequently targeted for sanctions.

For example, you may decide that a risk is low if it involves a loss of under five thousand dollars, does not require reporting to OFAC, and is unlikely to be publicized. On the other hand, you may decide a risk is high if it would involve a penalty of over $1 million, lead to potential lawsuits, and be publicized globally.

Making this assessment more complicated, a spectrum of risks may be identifiable within the same category. For example, some customers (individuals) may be at lower risk than others (military customers). This is why it's essential to try to quantify these risk categories. If 95 percent of your customers are individuals, your customer risk will be lower than if 95 percent of your customers are military customers.

For those without prior experience with risk assessments, the Federal Financial Institutions Examination Council (FFIEC)[22] BSA/AML Manual provides a suitable, easy-to-read matrix that categorizes activities as high, medium, or low risk. OFAC also uses this matrix.[23]

Let's break it down for the examples above.

Barb's Baubles

Customers: low risk

In general, individuals are lower-risk customers absent other information about the customer base. Higher-risk customers will try to hide behind entities and layers of entities. Barb's Baubles has 50 percent repeat customers and a somewhat stable customer base, which is lower risk as they've done business with these customers before and know their purchase and spending patterns (the better to identify anomalies).

Product: low risk

Moderately priced jewelry isn't a high-risk product. However, if they were to deal in the luxury jewelry market, the risk would be higher, as high-end jewelry can be used for money laundering or attracting high-risk customers.

Services: medium risk

Selling entirely online increases risk because you don't have direct, face-to-face interactions with your customers. While payment service providers (PSPs) are also responsible for reviewing their users, weaknesses in their controls have led to fines for sanctions violations.[24] Sanctioned parties often prefer these payment services because they have weaker customer due diligence than banks.

Geography: medium risk

Conducting worldwide sales online also brings geographic risk, as they may not know precisely where their customers are located, and thus, they could inadvertently sell to a customer in a sanctioned country. Larger companies will employ IP (internet protocol) blocking to keep those customers from making a transaction, but smaller companies, such as Barb's Baubles, likely won't have that tool. People residing in countries with trade embargos frequently employ virtual private networks (VPNs) to get around IP blocking, too.

The assessment of Barb's Baubles' overall sanctions risk is medium-low.

ABC Company

Customers: medium-high to high risk

Most of ABC Company's customers are businesses, including wholesalers, who can distribute their product to anyone, even to parties or countries restricted by OFAC. Assessing customer risk as high or medium-high depends on whether they have a stable customer base or a variety of one-time customers. Products sold through sales offices pose a lower risk because sales staff know their customers well and understand their needs and typical transactions.

Product: high risk

The product is computer parts, which fall into a category frequently restricted by OFAC across various sanctions programs. These goods are often used in sanctioned industries, such as the military and defense.

Geography: high risk

ABC Company operates worldwide, with activities in two higher-risk countries—China and India—and sales offices in ten other countries. Their assessment revealed that only 25 percent of their product may be sold in higher-risk countries like China, which can lower the overall global risk. However, their wholesalers, whether domestic or foreign, can sell anywhere to customers and countries unknown to ABC Company.

Services: high risk

Their services are higher risk, especially those involving extending credit, using payment services, or accepting cryptocurrency. Cryptocurrency is the highest-risk service because it is often used by criminals due to its anonymity.

The assessment of ABC Company's overall sanctions risk is high.

Identify All Sanctions Risks

Now that you have assessed your company's baseline risk based on your customers, products, locations, and services, you need to identify the specific sanctions-related risks for your company. Brainstorm all the ways your organization could violate sanctions without any controls in place. This will be your universe of risks that you have to mitigate.

When framing risks, ensure they are not phrased as broken controls (i.e., a missing or defective control). For example, "the risk that we don't scan our customers" is not a risk but a broken control. Not performing a control (scanning) is a gap, not a risk. Instead, the risk is "sanctioned customers are not identified" or "we do business with sanctioned parties." Scanning would be a way to control those risks.

Some sanctions risks that your company may face include (this is not an exhaustive list):

- The company's sanctions compliance program is insufficient to comply with economic sanctions.
- The company does not identify sanctions issues.
- Sanctioned customers are not identified.
- Transactions that violate sanctions are conducted.
- Employees don't understand sanctions.
- New sanctions requirements are not identified and implemented.
- Third parties may put the company at risk for sanctions violations.

Identify Controls

Once you've assessed the sanctions-related risks, you need to identify and evaluate the controls (i.e., processes and procedures) that reduce those risks, if they exist. If you are starting to develop a sanctions program, you may not have any controls in place yet, or there may be controls throughout the company that you haven't identified.

Chapter 6 will discuss controls in more detail, but here are examples of controls you may have for the risks from the last section.

The company does not identify sanctions issues.

- sanctions program
- economic sanctions policy
- sanctions compliance officer
- employee training
- risk assessment

Sanctioned customers are not identified.

- Customers are screened at onboarding and periodically after that using an automated system.
- Customer due diligence, including a beneficial ownership review, is conducted at account opening.

Transactions that violate sanctions are conducted.

- OFAC watchlist screening of all payment transactions using an automated system.
- Manual screening of all wire payments by accounts payable before their release to the bank.
- Contract provisions prohibit certain activities by vendors, wholesalers, and other third parties doing business on the company's behalf.

Employees don't understand sanctions.

- Annual training is required for all staff.
- Other communications, such as e-newsletters or articles, are posted periodically on an internal shared online site (such as SharePoint).

New sanctions requirements are not identified and implemented.

- Environmental scanning identifies new sanctions requirements.

Third parties may put the company at risk for sanctions violations.

- Vendor due diligence is conducted at onboarding.
- Ongoing monitoring of vendors for new sanctions issues is carried out.

Assess Controls

Once you've identified all applicable sanctions-related controls, you should assess whether they are working properly and are strong enough to fully mitigate the sanctions risk. Use the following criteria for your controls assessment:

Inherent Risk

Inherent risk is the sanctions risk level—high, medium, or low—before implementing any controls. In simpler terms, it's how likely sanctions violations will occur if there are no controls. For example, a company like ABC Company, with high-risk factors in its customers, products, services, and geography, might have a high inherent risk level for the sanctions risk, "sanctioned customers are not identified." In contrast, Barb's Baubles might have a medium inherent risk for this same risk.

Control Effectiveness

Effectiveness asks if the control functions properly. Does it work consistently, occasionally, or not at all? Or is there no control in place? A risk is only reduced if the control is both in place and working effectively. A control can be evaluated as "effective," "partially effective," or "ineffective." A partially effective control is in place and somewhat functional, but a gap may still exist. For instance, the claims team might manually scan many, but not all, wire payments before sending them out. An ineffective control isn't performed or doesn't work more often than not.

Residual Risk

Residual risk is the likelihood—high, medium, or low—that a sanctions violation will occur after the controls are implemented. Your goal is that the controls will reduce the inherent risk of a sanctions risk. A company with a high inherent risk for "sanctioned customers are not identified" may find that with robust, effective controls in place, their residual risk falls to medium or even low. A company with few or ineffective controls may find that the residual risk remains high.

If the sanctions risk remains outside of your risk tolerance (i.e., a residual risk of high or even medium) with the current controls, then procedures must be revised to be more effective, or different processes must be developed. However, your goal is not to completely eliminate all risk, as that would not be possible.

Third Parties and Controls

A control that an external party performs for you is not a control for your program. You can't depend solely on an external third party, like a bank, to carry out a control for you. Instead, you must either (1) perform the control yourself (such as screening a payee before sending a payment to the bank) or (2) oversee the third party's completion of the control procedure. For example, as part of your compliance testing program, you may periodically audit payments made by a third-party vendor to ensure they are being properly screened. While you can acknowledge in the risk assessment that a third party performs a control, your company's control involves overseeing the third party's actions. OFAC doesn't permit a company to rely solely on a third party to fulfill its sanctions requirements without oversight.[25]

Identifying Gaps and Potential Resolutions

Now that you've identified and assessed the sanctions controls in place, you've arrived at the critical part of the risk assessment: What are your control gaps, why do those gaps exist (i.e., the root cause), and what can you do to close those gaps?

A control gap happens when the controls don't operate well or are missing altogether. You have a control gap if you have a sanctions risk with no control to mitigate it.

The first step to remedy this gap is to figure out why it happened. You may hear this referred to as a "root cause analysis." Perhaps procedures are outdated, technology is insufficient, resources are inadequate to perform the tasks, or the procedure was dropped when a function was reorganized. All of those can be reasons why a control gap exists. Just ask "why?" to conduct the analysis.

The last step is to close the gap by redesigning the control or implementing a new one.

Let's conduct an example root cause analysis.

In your risk assessment, you identify that your employees weren't manually scanning payees before sending a wire to a bank. That's the gap. When you ask why, you find out it's because they didn't know they were supposed to. When you ask why again, you learn they haven't been trained on the procedure and don't know what sanctions are. In fact, you discover that no one has trained them on sanctions for at least five years. That's the root cause of the problem. To fix it, you create a training program to educate employees on sanctions in general and the manual scanning procedure specifically.

How Do I Know What Countries Are High Risk?

While examining the sample assessments provided earlier, you might be curious about how to identify which countries pose higher risks. There are several methods to consider, and a country that ends up being rated high risk according to one or more of these methods should be considered the highest risk:

- Countries with OFAC sanctions programs[26] should be considered higher risk. Those countries with trade embargoes—Iran, Syria, Cuba, North Korea, and Russian-held regions of Ukraine, such as Crimea—are the highest risk, as most business activity in these countries is prohibited. Also, consider those countries that are allied with these highest-risk countries. For example, China and India are friendly toward Russia. Although India doesn't have a sanctions program, it may be considered a higher risk than a country such as the UK.
- The Financial Action Task Force (FATF)[27] lists countries on "black" and "gray" lists for anti-money laundering deficiencies. These countries can be considered higher-risk due to their lack of controls over fraud and abuse. Currently, Iran, Myanmar, and North Korea are on the black list.
- Transparency International[28] is a great resource that calculates a corruption index and ranks countries based on their level of corruption. Download their Corruption Perceptions Index spreadsheet to identify if a country you are doing business in is considered corrupt. According to their 2024 index, Denmark is the least corrupt country, while South Sudan is the most corrupt.

- Current events should also factor into your geographic risk analysis. While there are no sanctions programs over Israel, the fact that it is a current political hot spot should move it toward the top of your risk list if you do business there.

Risk Assessment Documentation

A risk assessment should be documented and updated at least annually or when there is a significant change to customers, products, services, or locations. For example, we revised the risk assessment when we acquired a foreign entity and again when Russia invaded Ukraine.

Generally, a risk assessment should be shared with management, such as the CCO, and the progress of gap remediation is also typically reported to upper management.

For a deeper dive into completing your company's risk assessment, review The Plain-English Guide to Economic Sanctions Risk Assessments and its companion workbook.

6
Internal Controls

Ensuring you have the proper controls to adequately address sanctions risk is crucial for your program's success. Without appropriate and effective safeguards, your program will not succeed, and your company could face fines and penalties. If you are just starting to develop a sanctions program, you may not have any controls in place yet. Or controls might be scattered throughout the company.

What Are Controls?

Internal controls are the processes, procedures, and measures that prevent and detect sanctions violations. Internal controls will reduce your sanctions risks. You may have a good idea of what controls exist within the company from your risk assessment.

What Controls Should Be Implemented?

Your controls will vary depending on your industry, size, and global scope.

- a written sanctions program
- an economic sanctions policy
- program oversight
- automated scanning/screening of customers and transactions
- customer due diligence
- third-party due diligence
- training
- contract language
- risk assessment
- auditing and testing
- written procedures
- environmental scanning

If these sound familiar, it's because other chapters explained in detail why they're key to a strong sanctions program. Those chapters also covered how to implement these controls effectively. If any are missing, it creates a weak spot in your program called a **control gap**.

Third Parties and Controls

A control that an external party performs for you is not a control for your program. You can't depend solely on an external third party, like a bank, to carry out a control for you. Instead, you must either (1) perform the control yourself (such as screening a payee before sending a payment to the bank) or (2) oversee the third party's completion of the control procedure.

For example, as part of your compliance testing program, you may periodically audit payments issued by a vendor to ensure they are being properly screened. While you can acknowledge in the risk assessment that a third party performs a control, your company's control is overseeing the vendor's actions. OFAC doesn't permit a company to rely solely on a third party to fulfill its sanctions requirements without oversight.[29]

Technology Is Key

Remember those "adequate resources" senior management is expected to provide to the sanctions compliance function? A sanctions compliance program will not be effective if it relies only on manual controls. People make mistakes, and manual work requires more staff. That's why automated procedures and applications are essential tools for sanctions compliance. Some processes that may require automation to be an effective control include:

- Scanning System - This is the number one technology a sanctions compliance program needs. See Chapter 8 for more information on vetting a screening application for purchase.
- Environmental Scanning - While a spreadsheet can be used to document the environmental scan process for smaller companies, a risk management system, such as Archer (https://www.archerirm.com/), which we used, would be more effective for larger companies.
- Risk Assessment - While a spreadsheet can be used to document the risk assessment process for smaller companies, a risk management system, such as Archer, which we used, would be more effective for larger companies.
- Training Platform - An automated training platform (i.e., a learning management system) can maintain your sanctions training course,

update it easily, automatically roll it out to large groups, and track who has completed it and when. Smaller companies may be able to do this manually, however, if needed.

- Document Management System - Nowadays, most documents and emails are kept digitally rather than on paper. A document management system is beneficial because it can automatically store documents securely, making them easily accessible to all employees within the company. These systems also automatically back up documents to ensure their safety. Sanctions-related documents must be retained for a minimum of ten years.

7

Due Diligence

A company should conduct two types of checks to identify potential sanctions issues before proceeding with business: one for its customers and another for its third-party business partners.

Customer Due Diligence

Customer due diligence means getting to know your customers to understand their risks. This includes the following procedures:

- checking a customer's name against sanctions watchlists
- finding out who owns and runs the customer's business (beneficial ownership)
- scanning beneficial owners' names against sanctions watchlists
- looking for any sanctions-related red flags in their business activities (such as geographic location)
- searching for any negative news about the customer, like past sanctions fines, or if they have connections to sanctioned parties

If your company has an Anti-Money Laundering Program, it likely already has customer due diligence procedures, including a sanctions check you can leverage.

Next, we'll explore two key challenges in customer due diligence.

Legal Entities and Ultimate Beneficial Ownership (UBO)

Various legal entities, such as limited liability companies (LLCs), limited partnerships (LPs), limited liability partnerships (LLPs), and public limited companies (PLCs), are commonly used by sanctioned parties to conceal their assets. These entities often obscure ownership details, especially when incorporated in jurisdictions such as Jersey or the Cayman Islands, which have opaque registration rules. Sanctioned individuals may further complicate matters by structuring these entities to be owned by other entities, making it challenging to uncover the true ownership.

Some companies, such as Dow Jones and Lexis Nexis, have compiled databases of the ultimate beneficial owners of various legal entities. Additionally, entities are now required to file beneficial ownership information with the Financial Crimes Enforcement Network (FinCEN) under the Beneficial Ownership Information Reporting Rule.[30]

However, these databases aren't infallible. When dealing with customers operating under one of these legal entities, requesting information and documentation of ultimate beneficial ownership during customer due diligence is essential to ensure compliance and avoid engaging with sanctioned parties. Russian oligarchs, in particular, use these vehicles to hide assets, ownership, and control of their businesses.

Politically Exposed Persons (PEPs)

Politically Exposed Persons (PEPs) add another layer of complexity to customer due diligence. A PEP is someone who holds a high-ranking public position in a domestic or foreign government—this includes presidents, judges, and heads of government agencies. Some regulators also classify close family members and associates of PEPs as PEPs due to their potential influence.

PEPs are considered high-risk customers, not because of sanctions compliance, but due to their position and the potential for corruption. However, some high-ranking officials, such as heads of state, may also appear on OFAC's sanctions lists.

OFAC does not require companies to screen for PEPs, but identifying them is integral to an effective customer due diligence program. In the US and many other countries, AML (anti-money laundering) regulations mandate the identification and enhanced monitoring of PEPs. If your company is subject to AML regulations, you should already be conducting these checks.

A key challenge with PEP screening is determining how long someone remains a PEP after leaving office. There is no universal standard, but a common guideline is two years.

We screened for PEPs using our sanctions screening system. While OFAC does not provide a PEP list, most screening vendors include one. Doing business with a PEP is not prohibited, but you should carefully assess any corruption or AML red flags, especially regarding their transactions or source of funds.

Most regulations focus on foreign PEPs, not domestic ones. We initially monitored both but found that tracking US PEPs generated a high volume of alerts with little value—after all, PEPs need insurance, too.

Third-Party Due Diligence

Similar due diligence steps should be taken with vendors and third parties, such as wholesalers, suppliers, and distributors. As part of your vendor contracting process, request the following information to vet for any sanctions issues:

- name and location of the company
- ownership of the company
- ultimate beneficial owners of the company (if different from ownership)
- if any executives or board members are on any sanctions watchlists
- which countries they will be working on your company's contract in
- any sanctions-related investigations, fines, or judgments in the last five years

In addition to reviewing the vendor's answers to these questions, you should conduct an independent negative news search for any sanctions-related issues in the last five years.

Realize that some companies will use subsidiaries or branches in other countries to perform the contract work. You need to identify those countries to verify that they do not have trade embargoes or other sanctions issues.

However, vendor management doesn't end after the contracting phase. If the contract with the vendor lasts for several years, it is essential to perform ongoing monitoring. The frequency will depend on the vendor's risk. Less frequent monitoring can be done on smaller contracts with US companies. More frequent reviews (such as annually) should be conducted for large contracts where companies perform key activities (such as payment processing) overseas. During your periodic monitoring, verify that the information gathered at onboarding is up-to-date, rescan all the names against the watchlists, conduct a negative news review for the time since onboarding, and verify that the countries where the work is being performed have not become sanctioned.

8

Setting Up a Scanning Program

Most emphasis on complying with sanctions is on scanning, also known as screening. Scanning involves checking a party's name against sanctions watchlists to see if there is a match. Surprisingly, OFAC does not require anyone to scan their business. However, no compliance program would be effective without it.

Sanctions Screening Program

The sanctions screening program should be in writing and consist of the following elements:

- the criteria an automated sanctions screening solution should include
- the sanctions watchlists to include in your scanning program
- what parties and transactions will be scanned
- what threshold(s) will be used to scan data
- how often data will be scanned
- when manual scanning should be conducted
- how potential matches will be cleared or escalated
- how to handle positive matches
- periodic testing of the application to ensure it's functioning as expected

Automated Scanning Application

An automated scanning application is the best way to implement a sanctions screening program, as once it's appropriately set up, it should operate with only minimal intervention. Once it's set up correctly, it requires minimal effort to keep it running. Instead of relying solely on manual scanning, which is time-consuming and prone to mistakes, an automated system lets you focus on reviewing potential matches only, rather than sorting through every transaction.

Some companies that offer sanctions screening applications include Lexis Nexis, Moody's, and Computer Services, Inc. (CSI).

When vetting a system, you should ask:

- What watchlists do you provide? Some companies offer hundreds of lists from around the world, including non-sanction lists, such as those excluding individuals from federally funded healthcare programs. This might be too much for your company. On the other hand, a smaller vendor might only provide US sanctions lists when you need global lists, too.
- Does the vendor keep the sanctions lists up-to-date, or do you? Most vendors will keep the watchlists updated themselves. If you use lists in addition to those provided by the vendor, you may be required to update them, which can be a hassle.
- How soon after a list is updated is your system updated? Same-day updating is ideal. OFAC has sanctioned companies for conducting transactions with a party that was sanctioned on the same day the transaction was made.[31]
- Do they use "fuzzy logic" to identify matches? Fuzzy logic involves using variations in spelling, phonetics, and name transposition (such as switching the first and last names) to identify potential matches.
- Can clearing logic be recorded in the system? Clearing logic is how you determine that a potential match is a false positive and not an actual match. It's important to document your reasons for clearing a match in the system, so you have proof if questions come up later.
- Can documents be attached in the system? If you use documents to clear an alert, you will want to attach them to the alert for future reference.
- Can you scan data against different watchlists and different thresholds depending on what the data is? Depending on your size and the data you want to scan, you may not want to screen all your data against the same watchlists at the same threshold. If you have both international and domestic business, you may want to screen the domestic business only against US lists while screening the international business against global lists.
- How long do you retain the alerts, clearing reasons, and attached documents? Data should be accessible for at least ten years in case you need to provide information to OFAC or auditors and to comply with OFAC's data retention requirements.

- Is there a whitelist or "good customer list" you can add people to? Once you clear a customer as a match to a sanctioned party, you don't want to look at that alert again. A whitelist or good customer list allows you to add these false positives to a list, so they won't alert again if rescanned unless they match a new sanctioned party.
- Is the system user-friendly? Is it easy to determine which of your customers is a potential match and to whom they are a match? Your customer can match to multiple people on the sanctions lists, and you'll need to identify, review, and clear each one individually.
- Is it easy for our data files to be loaded and scanned through the system? It would be best to set up a system to automatically feed new data files into the screening system.

What Data Should Be Scanned?

Everyone you do business with should be scanned. This includes:

- all customers (including joint accountholders or multiple insureds under an insurance policy)
- beneficiaries of accounts
- payees to whom checks are issued
- payors who make a payment or deposit on an account
- employees
- vendors
- other business partners, such as attorneys
- third-party claimants (for example, under an auto policy or a loss adjustor)
- joint venture partners
- merger and acquisition targets
- counterparties of trades

If you ship goods, the list of participants who should be scanned is even longer, including:

- purchaser
- seller
- shipper
- shipping company
- vessel name

- consignee
- freight forwarder
- the ultimate beneficiary of the shipment
- countries through which the shipment is transiting
- goods shipped

If you sell high-risk or dual-use goods, you should screen them against their destination to ensure they are not prohibited from being exported there.

Finally, you should also scan the countries in which you are doing business to ensure they are not the target of a trade embargo.

OFAC considers an entire transaction prohibited if even one party to it is sanctioned.

How Do We Scan This Data?

If you have multiple systems with data (i.e., customers in one database, payments flowing through another), you'll need to figure out how to extract data from each system to feed through your sanctions screening application. Your IT person should be your initial contact for this task. They'll understand the data that can be extracted, how to do it, and how to format it into a file that can be uploaded and scanned into your sanctions screening application. Most systems allow uploads in Excel, comma-delimited text files, or similar formats.

Larger organizations can arrange real-time scanning by connecting their system, such as a payment system, to the sanctions screening application using an API (Application Programming Interface). This connection instantly checks payee or customer names entered into the system against the sanctions screening application, giving immediate results (match or no match).

Our company set up an internal website with an API that let employees screen names against a select group of global watchlists. This helped staff quickly check wire payments or new business without sending it to sanctions compliance and waiting for a response, saving time for everyone.

For situations where data cannot be automatically scanned or scanned promptly, manual scanning can be conducted. OFAC offers manual scanning of its lists through the OFAC website: https://sanctionssearch.ofac.treas.gov/.

How Often and When Should Data Be Scanned?

How often and at what point you scan your data depends on the level of risk involved. For example, a business selling jewelry online might only need to check a customer's name when processing payments. However, companies that manage accounts, like banks or insurers, should screen transactions as they happen and periodically rescan their entire customer list.

In general, OFAC will expect you to scan data **before**:

- onboarding a new customer
- issuing a policy
- sending a payment
- conducting a transaction
- receiving a payment and depositing it into your account
- signing a contract
- renewing a contract or policy
- shipping goods

For businesses managing accounts, periodic rescans are necessary, even if no transactions have occurred recently, as OFAC prohibits maintaining accounts, contracts, or policies with sanctioned parties.

This doesn't mean you need to screen your data daily. While OFAC updates its watchlists regularly, it's not a daily occurrence. However, OFAC requires that your watchlists stay up-to-date and that you rescan them immediately after any updates. Most automated systems will update your data within 24 hours of a watchlist change.

How often you run scans depends on risk. Some information, like new accounts or payments, should be scanned daily. Higher-risk records, such as those of foreign customers, should be rescanned daily or whenever the lists are updated. Lower-risk categories, like domestic vendors, can be checked monthly or at another appropriate interval.

Many automated screening systems maintain a customer database. This allows the system to automatically rescan all parties when sanctions lists (such as those from the US or the UK) are updated. The database is built by storing every scanned item for ongoing monitoring.

This practice helps ensure compliance and protects your company from inadvertently working with sanctioned parties.

What Sanctions Lists Should We Use?

If you operate solely domestically (no foreign customers, employees, or vendors), you can use OFAC's sanctions lists. However, OFAC maintains several watchlists: SDN lists (parties with full blocking prohibitions) and non-SDN lists (parties with other targeted restrictions). Whenever your transaction has a US nexus, you should ensure your scanning system screens them all.

If you have any foreign business, customers, or business partners, you should include the foreign government sanctions watchlists for relevant countries. Most countries have their own lists, but you may not do business in all those countries. Some top picks are Canada, the UK, the EU, and Australia. A comprehensive global sanctions dataset is necessary for companies operating in multiple countries. Dow Jones offers a list that can be integrated into your screening solution as an additional watchlist.

If you deal in goods (buying, shipping, distributing, or insuring), you must also scan the BIS and DoS lists for parties prohibited from exporting US-origin goods. A consolidated list where you can manually scan all these lists at once is located here: https://www.trade.gov/consolidated-screening-list. Otherwise, most sanctions application vendors will include those lists in their datasets that are available for scanning.

What Threshold Should We Use?

A threshold is the level at which the sanctions screening application considers a party a potential match to a sanctioned party. For example, your customer "Jose C. Rodriguez" may match against "Jose Rodrigues" or "Jose P Rodriguez" at a 95 percent threshold.

The threshold you use will depend on your application testing, which is discussed later in this chapter. You probably won't want to set all of your thresholds to 100 percent (exact name matches), but you also don't want them set so low (such as 85 percent) that you get hundreds of false positives to sift through. Higher-risk data, such as foreign customers, should generally be scanned at a lower threshold to capture name variations.

For example, Hispanic customers may have two last names (the father's surname and the mother's surname), which they may not use consistently.

Asian customers might list their surname first and their given name second. A lower threshold will account for these variations (i.e., via "fuzzy logic").

How Should We Clear Potential Matches?

There are many common names on the OFAC lists, so you will likely find a customer who is a name match to an SDN. For example, the name "Jose Rodriguez" will produce nine hits at a 100 percent threshold. Are any of these hits positive matches?

Matches are usually determined to be a "false positive" (i.e., not an actual match) after comparing your customer information to the information on the SDN provided by OFAC. Obtain information from your customer, such as Social Security Number, Date of Birth, and address history, that you can compare to the party on the SDN list to clear this potential match.

Define what criteria you will use to clear an alert. For example, do you rely solely on name, address, and date of birth, or can you use a customer's social media profile picture to estimate their age compared to the sanctioned party? Additionally, specify how many criteria must match to deem it a positive match—name only, name and address, name and date of birth, or all three?

Remember, people move, so not having a match on the address is usually insufficient to clear an alert. You may want to review their address history (obtained from the customer or a public records search, such as LexisNexis) to verify how long they've lived at certain addresses and whether they've ever lived in the same state or country as the sanctioned party.

I don't recommend using photos to clear an alert, as you don't know how old the images are. Use self-reported information, such as on Facebook or LinkedIn, sparingly and only if you can verify it is your customer's profile, not someone with the same name.

You can also search for information on public sites, such as occupational licenses, home ownership records, and tax records, to find details about your customer that can help clear a false positive. News articles showing your sanctioned party operating in a different occupation in a different country from your customer can also help clear a potential match.

If you struggle to clear a match, contact OFAC for guidance. OFAC prefers companies not report matches unless they are confident it's positive.

If your customer's information doesn't agree with the SDN details, it's probably safe to clear the alert as a false positive.

Do I Need to Document This?

Yes, keep records of how you confirmed someone isn't a match to the SDN. You may need this information if they appear again as a match or if you are asked about it. In my previous role, banks often asked about customers we initiated transactions for who popped up on their sanctions check system. Most automated scanning applications will have space to document your clearing reasons and allow you to attach relevant documentation.

Written Procedures for Sanctions Screening

Any procedures supporting sanctions-related processes should be in writing. This shows OFAC, auditors, and internal parties like the CCO that procedures are in place and how they work, serving as a valuable training tool for new staff.

Here's a list of procedures you may consider implementing in your company. The specific procedures you choose will depend on your company's risk level, size, and scope of operations:

- How the sanctions compliance team will review and clear potential alerts generated by the system. Your procedures should outline the criteria for clearing an alert and specify how many criteria must match to deem it a positive match.
- How and when potential sanctions issues should be escalated to the sanctions compliance officer for review.
- How positive matches are handled, including rejecting transactions, blocking assets, or dissolving the business relationship.
- How positive matches, rejected transactions, blocked property, and possible violations are reported to OFAC.
- When other staff within the company should refer a transaction or account to sanctions compliance for review.

You may want to document (a spreadsheet will do) what data is scanned, what internal system the data is from, what watchlists and thresholds are used, how frequently the data is screened, and your reasoning for these parameters. This will help track that you are scanning all necessary data and assist in the risk assessment.

Periodic Testing of the Application

It's important to periodically test your scanning application to ensure it's functioning as expected. Vendors often update their scanning engines, especially their fuzzy logic, which can affect the quality of alerts over time.

When to Test

- Test the system when it's first set up.
- Test periodically based on risk, but at least once every three to five years.
- Test when there are significant changes in your company's operations, like acquiring a foreign entity with higher-risk business.

How to Test

- Feed test data through your application to see what alerts appear at different threshold levels.
- Use sanctioned party data from various OFAC and global watchlists.
- Adjust entries (transpose names, misspell names, change residence countries, etc.) and scan them at different thresholds (such as 90 percent, 95 percent, and 99 percent).
- Evaluate the alerts at each threshold, looking for quality alerts you'd expect to review, not just positive matches. Also, look for alerts you expected to receive but did not.
- Scan current "live" data files (i.e., actual business data) at the same thresholds and watchlists to compare results. This will help you calibrate the system for your business.

Evaluate Results

- Determine if any watchlists need to be changed based on the test results.
- Find the threshold that provides the best mix of quality alerts and minimal false positives. Avoid using a threshold that generates mostly false positives just to catch a rare misspelled sanctioned party name.

Documentation

Document your testing process, results, changes made, and approvals received. This ensures you have a record of your methods and decisions, which is crucial for compliance and future reference.

Referral Process

While an automated scanning process goes a long way toward ensuring sanctions compliance, remember that scanning cannot be your only control. At my prior organization, staff believed that if we scanned customer names, we were in compliance with OFAC regulations. That is not the case. Scanning won't catch everything.

Not all transaction details needing review may pass through your sanctions screening program. For instance, let's say you have a product liability insurance policy for a US-based customer. The policy documents reveal that they sell their products in countries like Russia, China, and Cuba. While your system will scan the customer and related parties covered by the policy, it may not be able to capture, feed, and screen all countries covered by the policy. As a result, certain sanctions risks might be overlooked.

In another example, your customer in the UK has a US bank as a counterparty, and the transaction involves sending goods to Cuba. That data may not be input into your administrative system and may not be sent to your screening application.

That is why a referral process is so important!

Our automated system couldn't catch all the sanctions risks in the policies we wrote, so we set up a referral process for underwriters and claims handlers. For higher-risk policies and claims, we established a straightforward procedure for determining when and how to refer cases to the sanctions compliance team. We also trained them on this process and explained why it's crucial. Employee referrals and automated screening are essential to a company's sanctions screening program.

What transactions should you include in your referral program? Consider any risks associated with comprehensively sanctioned countries or higher-risk nations, such as Russia and Venezuela, where US sanctions differ from those of other countries. Staff will need a clear understanding of what constitutes a sanctions nexus. For the above examples, the underwriter of the product liability policy would refer the business as the customer wants to cover Cuban sales, and the employee setting up the Cuban transaction would refer the business because there is a US bank counterparty.

9

Written Sanctions Procedures

Any procedures supporting sanctions-related processes should be in writing. This shows OFAC, auditors, and internal parties like the CCO that procedures are in place and how they work, and it serves as a valuable training tool for new sanctions staff.

Here's a list of procedures you may consider implementing in your company. The specific procedures you choose will depend on your company's risk level, size, and scope of operations:

- how to review and clear alerts from a scanning application
- how and when to manually scan business
- when other departments need to refer business to the sanctions compliance team or the SCO for review
- what steps to take if a customer is sanctioned
- how to conduct a risk assessment
- how to stay updated on regulatory changes to OFAC programs
- how to escalate any sanctions issues (such as a potential violation)
- how and when to contact OFAC (filing blocked asset and rejected transaction reports, applying for specific licenses, filing a voluntary self-disclosure, etc.)

Best Practices for Procedures

Decide which processes need written procedures. Then, determine what staff members need to perform them. Do all of your sanctions procedures rest with the sanctions compliance team, or do employees in other departments also need written procedures for handling sanctions-related tasks? For example, if you have separate banking, treasury, or accounts receivable/accounts payable functions, they may need procedures for when to manually scan payees and payors. The CCO may need to review and provide input on the procedures for escalating sanctions issues. Other lines of business may need written guidelines on when to refer a transaction or piece of business to sanctions compliance for review.

Collaborate on procedures with the people who will be responsible for carrying them out. This lesson was hard-learned from my previous role.

When you create procedures solely based on your vision, they may not be feasible for the staff tasked with implementing them, and they will push back on doing them or not do them at all. Engage with the team from the start; they often have valuable insights on executing the procedures effectively. This approach ensures their initial support for the procedure and increases the likelihood of its success.

Although several departments may handle the procedures, it's crucial to have one person, such as the SCO, oversee all sanctions-related processes.

Some additional best practices for written procedures:

- Even though several departments may handle the procedures, it's crucial to have one person, like the SCO, oversee all sanctions-related processes.
- Maintain the documents in a common area (for example, an online shared site) so the most recent version can be easily accessed.
- Procedures should be reviewed and updated at least annually or when there is a significant update to a process.
- You may want to maintain a list of all your procedures with their current version number and the date they were last revised.

How to Write a Procedure

If you've never written a procedure before, it can be daunting. Below are some suggested ways to go about drafting your process document:

- Clearly title the document. What does this document cover? For example, "When to Refer a Transaction to Sanctions Compliance." It's clear that staff should consult this document to determine if a piece of business they are working on requires referral. Don't just title it "Referral Procedures," as that's vague. Refer to whom and for what?
- More critical procedures, especially those conducted by persons outside of the sanctions compliance team, may benefit from identifying the scope and purpose of the document. Why does this procedure exist, and who needs to follow it? For example, in the first bullet, the scope and purpose may be as follows: "This document will assist claims handlers in identifying when a claim needs to be referred to sanctions compliance for review before a payment is issued."

- A revision date and/or version number may be included so staff can easily identify that they are using the most current version.
- Who is responsible for the procedure? If you have a scope and purpose, this is probably already listed. If not, you can note that here. For example, "the sanctions compliance team is responsible for this process."
- Go step-by-step. This document will help train new staff and serve as a reminder to current staff of the correct procedures. If you can walk through the process first, that would be best. Don't skip any steps, even if they seem obvious, to avoid confusing the reader. Use clear and concise language. Organize the steps logically. Some people may begin by creating a high-level flowchart that shows how the process works.
- Use screenshots if the document explains how to use a system. For example, in a procedure detailing how to clear alerts in your sanctions screening system, include screenshots from your application to illustrate the steps. These screenshots could show where to find information, how to input clearing reasons, how to close alerts, and how to attach documents. It's much easier to show the appropriate tab to click with a screenshot rather than to describe how to find it in words.
- Remember to obtain input on the process from the people who will perform it and have them review it before you finalize it, in case something is unclear or you missed a step.
- Once it's finalized, distribute it to all staff who will perform the procedure and their managers and post it on your shared internal site for easy access to updates. Some teams may have their own process manuals to which the new procedure needs to be added. Provide training, if necessary, on the new process.

10
Sanctions Clauses

One of the most important tools for staying compliant with sanctions is including exclusion clauses in contracts and insurance policies. These clauses state that the contract or policy is void if a sanctions violation occurs, helping you avoid paying for or covering prohibited transactions. Another clause could prohibit the resale of your goods to countries where their sale is banned.

OFAC said, "The best and most reliable approach for insuring global risks without violating US sanctions law is to insert in global insurance policies an explicit exclusion for risks that would violate US sanctions law... It essentially shifts the risk of loss for the underlying transaction back to the insured - the person more likely to have direct control over the economic activity giving rise to the contact with a sanctioned country, entity, or individual."[32]

In reality, you must not engage in any transaction that violates economic sanctions, even if that's not explicitly stated in your contract. However, including such a clause can offer you legal protection in the event of a dispute, provide a basis for OFAC to reduce fines, and notify the contracted party that they will not be covered in situations where sanctions are violated.

You will want to enlist the services of an attorney to ensure that your sanctions clauses are valid and well-worded, thereby protecting you.

Sanctions exclusion language should be consistent across all documents and contracts to prevent gaps or discrepancies. You may want to include the approved exclusion language in your economic sanctions policy to ensure consistency.

Contracts

Several different types of contracts would benefit from a sanctions exclusion clause.

When contracting with a vendor for services, ensure the contract mandates compliance with sanctions and that they cannot become sanctioned or payment will not be made under the contract. Consider adding language requiring them to report any sanctions violations to you as part of your ongoing vendor monitoring process.

Similarly, if goods are sold to a third party, like a wholesaler, the contract should specify that the goods cannot be resold in a way that breaches sanctions, such as selling to a sanctioned party or country.

If your contract or the contract participants cover multiple jurisdictions, the sanctions exclusion clause should list the regions where a sanctions violation would void the contract. Clarifying which legal jurisdiction governs your contract is crucial because sanctions regulations vary between jurisdictions, affecting what's permissible. For instance, if you're under US jurisdiction and the transaction could breach US but not UK sanctions, you wouldn't want a clause that only covers compliance with UK sanctions regulations.

Typically, your sanctions exclusion clause would state that the contract becomes invalid if it breaches laws in any of these jurisdictions: your own, the contractor's, and the jurisdiction(s) where the transactions are conducted. Specifying these countries ensures that there's no debate about invoking the sanctions clause if an OFAC violation occurs.

Insurance Policies

For insurance companies, your policies should have language that excludes coverage for sanctioned parties or losses and prohibits claims payments if they violate sanctions.

There may be a sanctions exclusion clause in your own personal insurance policies.

We based the sanctions exclusion language in our policies on Lloyd's LMA3100 form[33]. Lloyd's is a London insurance market, and their sanctions exclusion language is widely accepted. The language basically states that the insurer isn't liable for any claim and is not required to provide coverage under the policy to the extent that it would expose the insurer to sanctions.

This language should be included in all policies, as an endorsement, or as a separate notice. How you incorporate the language depends on how easily your forms can be updated and whether those forms must be resubmitted for state review. You may want to use a notice, for example, if revisions to the form would cause a state to reopen and review the entire policy contract language, which could lead to a lot of avoidable work!

Sanctions Clauses Are Not Foolproof

Be aware, however, that sanctions clauses may not fully protect you in legal disputes.

The EU and the UK have "blocking statutes"[34] barring compliance with OFAC sanctions that conflict with their own (such as those for Iran and Cuba). This aims to protect UK and EU companies from extraterritorial laws, allowing them to conduct business freely.

While the UK and EU governments won't sue US companies for using sanctions clauses, affected companies can bring civil cases against them.

Recent court cases have shown mixed outcomes.

In 2018, the UK High Court ruled insurers aren't liable to pay a claim when payments violate sanctions laws.[35] The Court said the blocking statute did not apply as the sanctions exclusion clause was part of the contract; therefore, the defendant relied on complying with a contractual provision rather than US sanctions laws.[36]

However, the court also said the requirement to make the payment is only suspended, not eliminated. If sanctions regulations change in the future so that this is no longer a prohibited transaction, the transaction should be completed at that time. This could cause open claims or payments to linger indefinitely.

In 2019, the UK High Court ruled in favor of a defendant who refused to make a payment due to OFAC sanctions. The court stated that the policy was clear regarding sanctions compliance, and the insured party should have been aware of the risks involved.

In 2020, a UK bank ceased making interest payments to a lender in Cyprus because the lender's owner had been designated as an SDN by OFAC. As a result, the lender was considered sanctioned under the 50 Percent Rule, and the bank was worried about facing US secondary sanctions. The defendant used a nonpayment clause in the facility agreement to justify this action. The English Court of Appeal decided that the bank could rely on this nonpayment clause because US secondary sanctions were considered a "mandatory provision of law," as stated in the clause. In this case, the risk of breaching US secondary sanctions was enough to enforce the clause.[37]

In 2021, however, the EU Court of Justice ruled that companies under EU jurisdiction aren't allowed to take action to comply with US sanctions that violate the EU's blocking statute. The entity must prove it wasn't seeking to comply with US sanctions laws when it canceled the business but took action for another appropriate reason.[38]

While this section focuses on EU and UK blocking statutes, be aware that other countries, such as China, Canada, France, and Germany, also have blocking statutes. Their enforcement of these statutes may differ from that of the UK and the EU.

How to Protect Your Organization

To protect your company from blocking statutes, consider the following:

- Excluding certain jurisdictions in your contracts. Include territorial exclusion clauses in your contracts to prevent transactions in countries such as Iran or Cuba, in addition to sanctions exclusion clauses. This is particularly important if you are a foreign company and the transaction could have a US nexus.
- Relying on other contract clauses. Use general non-compliance with laws and regulations clauses or other legal grounds for ending a contract instead of citing sanctions.
- Carefully documenting your business decisions when canceling business due to sanctions. The documentation must show solid reasons for terminating a business, and these reasons must not show an intention to comply with US laws.
- Applying for a specific OFAC license. You might consider applying for an OFAC license to conduct the transaction. However, you must first obtain permission (i.e., a license) from the UK or EU authorities to apply for an OFAC license, and these applications are publicly available. If your customer sees you're trying to comply with US sanctions that conflict with UK or EU sanctions, it might sue you.

So, sanctions clauses can help your company avoid violations of OFAC sanctions and the associated fines, but they may not fully protect against lawsuits under other countries' blocking statutes.

11
Environmental Scanning

Think of environmental scanning (aka "e-scan") as how you, as the sanctions compliance professional, stay updated on changes in economic sanctions regulations.

Sanctions change regularly, so you must monitor them daily for updates to watchlists, changes to sanctions programs, or the implementation of new programs.

You should develop a written procedure that documents how you will conduct the scanning, record your findings, and develop and implement new processes in response to new regulations.

Documenting Your E-Scan

You should record the results of your e-scan. You can do this easily in a spreadsheet, or larger companies might have a risk management application you can use. Create a spreadsheet with columns for the date, the source, the title, a brief summary of the item, whether it's relevant to your company, whether the change is already in effect (some rules may start later), if procedures need updating, the plan to update them, and the date it's completed.

An example spreadsheet setup:

Item #	2024-01
Date	4/29/2024
Source	OFAC
Title	Issuance of Russia-related General License
Summary	GL 8I extended, allowing certain energy-related services to be provided to specific Russian companies.
Effective?	Yes
Applicable?	Yes
Procedure Updates Needed?	No
Plan	Contact staff to inform them that this license has been extended, and we can continue to use it.
Date Completed	5/1/2024

How to Conduct Environmental Scanning

Set up automatic emails so you don't have to resort to manual Google searches.

Some good places to get updates:

- Sign up at OFAC's website to get emails when they update lists and programs: https://service.govdelivery.com/accounts/USTREAS/subscriber/new.
- The UK's Office of Financial Sanctions Implementation (OFSI), which administers UK sanctions, also has an automated email system. You can sign up here: https://ofsi.blog.gov.uk/subscribe/.
- Join an organization. The Association of Certified Anti-Money Laundering Specialists (ACAMS) has a large sanctions team. Membership fees are nominal but provide a wealth of sanctions-related information, webinars, and conferences. https://www.acams.org/en.
- Set up Google alerts for keywords such as "sanctions," "OFAC," "economic sanctions," "trade sanctions," and "sanctions fines."
- Consider subscription services. Moneylaundering.com (a separate subscription service of ACAMS) collects news articles on sanctions, anti-money laundering (AML), and bribery and corruption from various sources. They send daily email summaries of new articles. While it can be costly, it's valuable for larger companies. Alternatively, you can subscribe to other services, such as Bloomberg or LexisNexis, which also provide sanctions-related articles and allow you to set up alerts.

Compliance Bulletins

Once you identify a relevant e-scan item, you should email the affected people in your company to inform them of how it affects them and their sanctions procedures. We referred to this email as a Compliance Bulletin and sent it to the applicable compliance professionals and line of business management. The Bulletin detailed the information in the spreadsheet above and may have listed required follow-up action by the parties who received the email (such as updating their processes). If you request that people take certain actions, work with them on those updates, and follow up later to ensure they were implemented.

Unless you have a small company with few people to update, it is best to use an automated risk management solution that will automatically send the bulletin to the relevant staff.

12
Training

A sanctions program will not be effective without staff training.

Per OFAC, training should (i) provide job-specific knowledge, (ii) communicate to each employee their sanctions compliance responsibilities, and (iii) hold employees accountable through testing.[39]

Who Needs Training?

Everyone in a company likely needs basic sanctions knowledge and training. Some employees who encounter sanctions issues regularly may require more detailed training. Your sanctions policy should describe who will receive sanctions training, who will provide it, how often it will be rolled out, and how completion will be tracked. Consider US sanctions-specific training for foreign staff in those jobs that frequently encounter US business.

Of course, the SCO and sanctions compliance staff will need training. However, their training will typically come from external sources, such as webinars and conferences. These sessions provide up-to-date, in-depth knowledge crucial for their roles.

Other jobs that may require at least a basic working knowledge of sanctions include those that (this is not an exhaustive list):

- process a payment (such as a claim, an account withdrawal, or vendor payment)
- originate a payment on an account
- open new accounts
- underwrite policies or loans
- process funds received from an external party or customer
- conduct customer due diligence
- import or export goods
- conduct marine shipments
- contract with vendors or other business partners
- hire staff
- sell products or services

Depending on your organization's size, you might collaborate with other business professionals in the line of business or compliance to decide which job roles need training. In larger companies, job titles can be generic, and these teams often have a deeper understanding of what each role entails and whether they would benefit from sanctions training.

You may also want to offer training to third-party providers who handle tasks such as customer account setup or payment services (i.e., job tasks with a higher risk of possible sanctions violations). Alternatively, review the training they offer their staff to ensure it meets your sanctions compliance needs. If you can't do this review, share your company's Vendor Code of Conduct outlining your expectations for sanctions compliance.

What Type of Training Should I Provide?

When you mention "training," many imagine being stuck in a stuffy room for hours. But that's not how it's done anymore. People are busy, and in larger companies, they often face frequent training requirements. Aim to make sanctions training quick and painless. Training can take various forms, all contributing to a robust sanctions training program.

A Formal Training Course

This will be the primary training for most company staff who require a basic understanding of sanctions. It can be conducted in person or online, using a PowerPoint course developed internally or an off-the-shelf program from a learning platform like Learning Pool (formerly True Office, https://learningpool.com/). Regardless of the format, the training should be brief, ideally lasting no more than thirty minutes. The exception is for staff regularly dealing with sanctions issues (see Internal Training Webinars). Online self-study courses should include a test or knowledge check questions that staff must pass to successfully complete the course.

After setting baseline expectations for staff regarding sanctions via this formal course, the following activities can be used for additional training refreshers throughout the year.

Team Meetings

Manager emails may suffice for minor procedural changes or regulatory updates. My organization sent periodic manager emails with updates on various topics, and we occasionally included sanctions updates. Managers then discuss the information in their next team meeting, ensuring it reaches all staff effectively.

Internal Training Webinars

You can hold periodic online live training sessions, like a Lunch and Learn. I've led sanctions-related sessions during these events. You can meet with specific groups to discuss sanctions issues relevant to them. These meetings might last up to an hour and provide detailed information tailored to higher-risk teams, such as those handling payments, account openings, policy underwriting, or claims processing.

E-Newsletters

Consider sending a regular sanctions e-newsletter to key staff members in your organization. It doesn't have to be frequent; every quarter or semi-annually may be sufficient. We did this at one time, but it was admittedly tough to keep the list current due to staff changes. However, it may work better for smaller organizations.

Online Articles/Blog

If your organization uses an internal Microsoft SharePoint site or a similar platform, it's a great place to share information. You can post a refresher article on sanctions (don't forget to link your sanctions policy!) or share updates on policies or upcoming training sessions. Sanctions compliance might even have a SharePoint-type site where staff can subscribe for updates. We used SharePoint for a sanctions "resource site," where we posted several sanctions-related documents that all staff could reference if they had questions. Our policy was posted there, along with slides from prior training, summaries of sanctions programs for the US, the UK, and the EU, a list of embargoed countries, and sanctions FAQs, among other documents.

How Often Should I Provide Training?

People in key roles with a sanction nexus need at least annual training and may also benefit from a refresher or more intensive training during the year. For those who just need to know the basics, a refresher every two to three years should do. Your risk assessment can help decide who needs training and how often.

How Should I Roll It Out?

You can issue your training using several methods. The method you use depends on several factors, including the size of your company, the number of employees requiring training, and the technology available to you.

- Automated rollout through a company's learning management system (LMS) is the easiest approach. Large companies often have an LMS for various training needs. You can integrate your sanctions training into this system, whether it's developed in-house or off-the-shelf. This system automatically assigns the course to the selected employees and sets a deadline, such as 30 days, for them to complete the training. It sends reminders if someone hasn't completed it on time. Plus, the course can include a test at the end for employees to pass, and the system tracks successful completion.
- A live online webinar is suitable for providing more detailed training on complex sanctions topics, targeting specific groups of employees. One positive is that this format allows the participants to ask clarifying questions of the presenter. You can also record these sessions for staff who couldn't make the live event or for new employees.
- A PowerPoint (or similar) presentation distributed manually can be challenging to manage, but is suitable for smaller organizations. You send the training materials via email to the relevant staff (or provide a link to a shared internal site where the training is located), set a completion deadline, and then they or their manager informs you when it's been completed.

How Should I Document Someone's Completed Training?

If you have an LMS, the system automatically records who took the training. Periodically, you should run a report of everyone to whom the training has been rolled out and see who has completed it and who is overdue (where you may want to personally follow up). The spreadsheet is your documentation of who received the training, in case someone requests it.

For online webinars, you typically send invitations to the affected parties. Then, you can see who attends the meeting and check them off the list. You can follow up with those who didn't participate in the webinar by sending a copy of the recording.

For manual rollout, use a spreadsheet to track all people assigned the training and when they complete it. You may also want to retain the emails you receive when someone reports they have completed the training, in case of questions.

13
Auditing/Testing

Auditing and testing are covered together in this chapter because they are both ways to ensure your program operates as expected. But they're actually two different processes, and you should use both to validate the effectiveness of your sanctions program.

Auditing

Audits check if current processes are working effectively and are consistent with the expected procedures. They help find weaknesses in the program and recommend ways to fix them.[40]

Auditing should be performed by someone outside of the sanctions compliance function. In most cases, the internal audit group conducts the audit; however, it can also be performed by external auditors or an internal compliance person who is not responsible for the program. Being independent allows for objectivity and a fresh perspective on the process.

Audits can be intensive and last for weeks. However, the good news is that sanctions compliance isn't usually audited annually. How often it happens depends on when the last audit was done, the results of that review, changes in risk, and the auditor's own assessment of the organization's risks (i.e., how sanctions risk compares to other risks within the company).

During the planning phase of the audit, the SCO and sanctions compliance team members will meet with auditors to discuss their processes and controls. They might walk the auditors through significant processes, like clearing alerts, and provide important documents, such as the policy and risk assessment. The auditors may create their own risk matrix or flowchart of the procedures and key controls.

At the end of the planning phase, the auditors will provide an engagement memo outlining the audit's scope and objectives. The scope is just the areas of the organization that the audit will cover. In this case, it may be the sanctions compliance function and related processes, such as a review of IT controls over the automated scanning system. The objectives are the auditors' goals for the audit. For example, one objective may be to evaluate whether the sanctions compliance program is sufficient to prevent the organization from conducting prohibited transactions.

Once the engagement memo is issued, audit testing will commence. Audit testing will likely include the following elements:

- reviewing the SCP documents, such as the policy, risk assessment, and key written procedures
- sample testing of certain transactions to ensure a sanctions scan was conducted
- sample testing of alerts to validate that they are cleared appropriately
- evaluating positive matches identified to verify they were handled according to written procedures
- reviewing a sample of oversight activities (such as compliance testing as discussed in the following section) to ensure they are being conducted

Expect to meet with the auditors occasionally throughout the audit to discuss any questions and findings they've identified to date. At the end of the audit, a closing meeting will be held, where auditors discuss their findings and suggest ways to fix any issues. "Findings" are simply potential weaknesses or gaps they've identified in the sanctions process, such as controls not performed consistently or being absent altogether.

Post-audit, the final report will be issued. Frequently, a rating of the sanctions compliance program will be included in the report. Potential ratings, which will vary by organization, include "effective," "partially effective," "significant improvement needed," and "ineffective." Obviously, you would rather have an effective program than an ineffective one. The audience for the report will usually include senior management. Sanctions compliance will be expected to remediate the gaps identified in the report, and the SCO should periodically report to senior management on the progress in resolving the findings.

Compliance Testing

Compliance testing differs from auditing in that it is ongoing and usually performed by the person responsible for overseeing the sanctions program. This person could be the SCO or, more commonly, the manager of the sanctions compliance team.

Compliance testing involves sample testing the performance of the internal controls to ensure they are functioning effectively. Your controls, and thus the tests you conduct, will vary, but below is a sample of some tests you may want to consider:

- review payment reports to ensure funds aren't being sent to sanctioned countries
- review a sample of cleared alerts to verify they are being reviewed within expected timeframes, the clearing reasons are accurate, items are escalated when needed, and relevant documentation is attached
- scan reports of new foreign accounts opened or policies issued to verify that there is no coverage for sanctioned countries
- analyze new vendor agreements, policies, or contracts to verify that sanctions exclusion language is included

You don't have to conduct every test each month. Set up a schedule based on risk. Perhaps you review a sample of cleared alerts monthly and perform one or two additional tests each quarter, for example.

You should document your review, perhaps with notes, initials, and date reviewed in reports or electronic documents.

14
Documentation

You may have noticed a recurring theme in this guide: every aspect of your sanctions compliance program must be thoroughly documented. This helps you keep track of decisions you made, controls you implemented, how alerts were cleared, what training was provided, etc., and goes a long way toward showing OFAC you have an effective program if there is a possible sanctions violation.

OFAC previously recommended keeping documentation for five years[41], but this requirement changed to ten years as of March 15, 2025.[42] If your company has been following the five-year rule, now is the time to inform affected staff (including those in other business units) to prevent premature document purging. Larger companies should also update their company-wide document retention policies to reflect this change.

If your company has a document management system, ensure that sanctions documents are being retained for at least ten years. Some documents, like those related to blocked property, may need to be kept indefinitely, as they may need to be referenced periodically. I occasionally referred to emails or documents older than ten years to refresh my memory about why and how we made certain decisions.

If you don't have a document management system, ensure your documents are stored on a server accessible to everyone and regularly backed up, with backups stored offsite or in the cloud when possible.

15

Penalties for Non-Compliance

OFAC is responsible for the civil enforcement of US sanctions laws and regulations. Violations can result in substantial fines, and civil and criminal penalties can exceed several million dollars.[43] Other governmental agencies, such as the Department of Justice (DOJ) or the New York Department of Financial Services, can also impose their own penalties for the same conduct.

Below are a couple larger fines that illustrate the extent to which a company may be subject to penalties.

British American Tobacco (BAT) settled with OFAC for $508 million for violations of the weapons proliferation and North Korea sanctions regulations. BAT is UK-based, and its foreign subsidiary in Singapore was also involved in these transactions, so they aren't automatically US persons for purposes of these regulations. However, the transactions had a US nexus, by use of a US correspondent banking account and a foreign branch of a US bank to clear these transactions.[44]

The largest fine to date, totaling $968 million, was imposed in November 2023 against Binance. Government agencies, including the Financial Crimes Enforcement Network (FinCEN), the Internal Revenue Service (IRS), and the Department of Justice (DOJ), were also involved. Binance got in trouble for not setting up systems to spot and report suspicious transactions involving terrorists, ransomware gangs, money launderers, and other criminals. OFAC said that Binance intentionally undermined and ineffectively implemented its own sanctions compliance controls.[45]

Besides fines, employees, officers, and directors face severe consequences, such as losing their jobs or facing jail time. The DOJ and the US Attorney might bring criminal charges. For instance, in 2022, a US citizen was sentenced to more than five years in prison. He violated sanctions laws by helping North Korea use blockchain and cryptocurrency to hide money and avoid US sanctions.[46]

In one final example, OFAC fined Navigators Insurance Company $272,000 for providing insurance to North Korean-flagged vessels. One of the factors contributing to this fine was the fact that it did not have a formal sanctions compliance program in place.[47]

It is important to note that OFAC operates on a strict liability basis. This means you can be fined for a violation of any amount (in theory, one dollar), even if you did not intend to violate sanctions. However, penalties will depend, in part, on the amount of the violation, whether it was inadvertent or deliberate, and whether you identified and reported the breach to OFAC.

You can significantly lower the fine if you self-report an identified violation to OFAC. OFAC considers non-reporting to be an aggravating factor that could increase your penalty. Binance, for example, did not self-report the violations to OFAC.

And don't overlook the damage to your reputation and your company's reputation when OFAC releases a press statement about your violation. Bad publicity and all the negative fallout from that violation can further harm your finances. Banks and other organizations may use this negative news to determine whether to work with you.

16
Conclusion

In the ever-evolving landscape of global commerce, navigating economic sanctions is crucial to doing business. Throughout this guide, we've explored the intricacies of developing an effective sanctions program. From setting up a policy, assessing your company's sanctions risks, and developing and implementing controls, this guide dove into the fundamental components and best practices necessary to ensure compliance with regulations set forth by the Office of Foreign Assets Control (OFAC).

Remember, compliance isn't just about avoiding fines but about upholding ethical and legal standards while navigating a complex global landscape. By adhering to sanctions regulations, your organization contributes to international stability and security, fostering a safer and more transparent economic environment.

Effective communication and collaboration across the company are essential. By involving key stakeholders in the development and implementation of sanctions compliance procedures, companies can ensure that policies are practical, executable, and aligned with business objectives. This collaborative approach fosters buy-in from employees at all levels and promotes a culture of compliance.

Additionally, leveraging technology and automation can streamline sanctions compliance processes and enhance efficiency. Technology provides valuable resources for effectively managing compliance obligations, including sanctions screening tools and automated reporting systems. By harnessing its power, companies can improve accuracy, reduce manual errors, and stay ahead of evolving regulatory requirements.

With dedication, diligence, and a commitment to excellence, you can build and sustain a robust sanctions program that safeguards your company's interests and promotes ethical business practices in today's interconnected world.

References

Below is a good list of websites with further details on the information provided in this guide.

All OFAC Sanctions Programs
https://ofac.treasury.gov/sanctions-programs-and-country-information

Federal Financial Institutions Examination Council (FFIEC), BSA/AML Manual, Appendix J: Quantity of Risk Matrix
https://bsaaml.ffiec.gov/manual/Appendices/11

FFIEC, BSA/AML Manual, Risk Assessment
https://bsaaml.ffiec.gov/manual/BSAAMLRiskAssessment/01

Free OFAC List Search Tool
https://sanctionssearch.ofac.treas.gov/

OFAC Compliance Guidance for Sanctions Programs
https://ofac.treasury.gov/media/16331/download?inline

OFAC Frequently Asked Questions
https://ofac.treasury.gov/faqs/all-faqs

Author Biography

Heidi Hunter worked for a US-based insurance company with global operations for over a decade. She developed and managed the company's sanctions compliance program, covering all its locations. She oversaw the team responsible for compliance with sanctions and worked closely with other teams within the company to ensure they understood and adhered to sanctions regulations. Heidi has a Master of Business Administration (MBA) and is a Certified Public Accountant (inactive).

Visit her website at https://easysanctions.wordpress.com/ for more information on sanctions and to sign up for her newsletter.

All Books in the Plain-English Guide Series by Heidi Hunter

The Plain-English Guide to Economic Sanctions
The Plain-English Guide to Developing an Economic Sanctions Program
The Plain-English Guide to Economic Sanctions Risk Assessments
The Plain-English Guide to Economic Sanctions for Insurance Companies
The Plain-English Guide to Economic Sanctions for Foreign Companies
The Plain-English Guide to Economic Sanctions: The Complete Series

Companion Workbooks:
The Plain-English Guide to Developing an Economic Sanctions Program Workbook
The Plain-English Guide to Economic Sanctions Risk Assessments Workbook

Book and Workbook Bundles:
The Plain-English Guide to Developing an Economic Sanctions Program: Full Guide & Workbook
The Plain-English Guide to Economic Sanctions Risk Assessments: Full Guide & Workbook

Find them all at: https://easysanctions.wordpress.com/books/

If you read one of my guides, please post a rating or review!

Notes

1. OFAC, Frequently Asked Questions, FAQ 12, https://ofac.treasury.gov/faqs/12.

2. Department of the Treasury, "A Framework for OFAC Compliance Commitments," https://ofac.treasury.gov/media/16331/download?inline.

3. Department of the Treasury, "A Framework for OFAC Compliance Commitments."

4. Following the end of Bashar al-Assad's regime, on January 6, 2025, OFAC issued General License 24, which expanded authorizations for activities and transactions in Syria for an initial six-month period, effective until July 7, 2025. This may lead to the permanent loosening of comprehensive sanctions against Syria.

5. OFAC, FAQ 986.

6. OFAC, FAQ 18.

7. OFAC, Frequently Asked Questions, FAQ 3, https://ofac.treasury.gov/faqs/all-faqs.

8. OFAC, FAQ 3.

9. OFAC, FAQ 886.

10. OFAC, FAQ 11.

11. OFAC, FAQ 10.

12. OFAC, FAQ 91.

13. Executive Order 13884, "Blocking Property of the Government of Venezuela," August 5, 2019, https://ofac.treasury.gov/media/26786/download?inline.

14. OFAC, FAQ 91.

15. Department of the Treasury, "Revised Guidance on Entities Owned by Persons Whose Property and Interests in Property Are Blocked," https://ofac.treasury.gov/media/6186/download?inline; OFAC, FAQ 399.

16. Department of the Treasury, "A Framework for OFAC Compliance Commitments," https://ofac.treasury.gov/media/16331/download?inline.

17. Department of the Treasury, "A Framework for OFAC Compliance Commitments."

18. Department of the Treasury, "A Framework for OFAC Compliance Commitments."

19. Department of the Treasury, "A Framework for OFAC Compliance Commitments."

20. Department of the Treasury, "A Framework for OFAC Compliance Commitments."

21. Vcomply, "What is a Risk Assessment Matrix? How to Create One?" accessed July 11, 2024, https://www.v-comply.com/blog/what-is-risk-assessment-matrix.

22. Federal Financial Institutions Examination Council (FFIEC), BSA/AML Manual, Appendix J: Quantity of Risk Matrix, accessed May 8, 2024, https://bsaaml.ffiec.gov/manual/Appendices/11.

23. OFAC, "OFAC Risk Matrix," Economic Sanctions Enforcement Guidelines, 31 C.F.R. Part 501, Appendix A, Annex, https://www.ecfr.gov/current/title-31/subtitle-B/chapter-V/part-501/appendix-Appendix_A_to_Part_501.

24. Department of the Treasury, "Settlement Agreement between the US Department of the Treasury's Office of Foreign Assets Control and PayPal, Inc.," March 25, 2015, https://ofac.treasury.gov/media/12326/download?inline.

25. FFIEC, BSA/AML Manual, Office of Foreign Assets Control, Office of Foreign Assets Control—Overview, accessed May 17, 2024, https://bsaaml.ffiec.gov/manual/OfficeOfForeignAssetsControl/01.

26. OFAC, Sanctions Programs and Country Information, https://ofac.treasury.gov/sanctions-programs-and-country-information.

27. FATF, "Black and Grey Lists," accessed May 20, 2024, https://www.fatf-gafi.org/en/countries/black-and-grey-lists.html.

28. Transparency International, Corruption Perceptions Index, https://www.transparency.org/en/cpi/2023.

29. FFIEC, BSA/AML Manual, Office of Foreign Assets Control,_Office of Foreign Assets Control—Overview, accessed May 17, 2024, https://bsaaml.ffiec.gov/manual/OfficeOfForeignAssetsControl/01.

30. FinCEN, Beneficial Ownership Information, Frequently Asked Questions, https://www.fincen.gov/boi-faqs.

31. Department of the Treasury, "OFAC Issues a Finding of Violation to MidFirst Bank for Violations of the Weapons of Mass Destruction Proliferators Sanctions Regulations", July 21, 2022, https://ofac.treasury.gov/media/924506/download?inline.

32. OFAC, FAQ 102.

33. Lloyds Market Association Bulletin LMA23-028-AR, "Sanctions Clauses," October 5, 2023, https://www.lmalloyds.com/LMA_Bulletins/LMA23-028-AR.aspx.

34. EU Council Regulation (E.C.) No 2271/96 of November 22, 1996, as amended by Commission Delegated Regulation (E.U.) 2018/1100 of June 6, 2018, https://www.legislation.gov.uk/eur/1996/2271; "Spotlight on the U.K. Protection of Trading Interests Legislation," Wilkie Compliance, accessed April 25, 2024, https://complianceconcourse.willkie.com/resources/sanctions-uk-uk-blocking-statute/.

35. Debevoise and Plimpton, "UK High Court Rules on Sanctions Clauses in Insurance Contracts and Considers Application of the EU Blocking Regulation," October 30, 2018, https://www.debevoise.com/-/media/files/insights/publications/2018/10/20181030_uk_high_court_rules_on_sanctions_clauses_in_insurance_contracts_and_considers_application_of_the_eu_blocking_regulation.pdf.

36. Debevoise and Plimpton, "UK High Court Rules on Sanctions Clauses in Insurance Contracts and Considers Application of the EU Blocking Regulation."

37. Royal Court of Justice, The Court of Appeal (Civil Division), Judgment, "Lamesa Investments Limited and Cynergy Bank Limited," June 30, 2020, https://www.judiciary.uk/wp-content/uploads/2020/07/Lamesa-v-Cynergy.APPROVED-JUDGMENTS.pdf.

38. Wilmer Hale, " Top EU Court Rules on the EU Blocking Regulation Against US Sanctions for the First Time," January 31, 2022, https://www.wilmerhale.com/insights/client-alerts/20220124-top-eu-court-rules-on-the-eu-blocking-regulation-against-us-sanctions-for-the-first-time.

39. Department of the Treasury, "A Framework for OFAC Compliance Commitments."

40. Department of the Treasury, "A Framework for OFAC Compliance Commitments."

41. *Code of Federal Regulations*, 31 CFR § 501.601 - Records and recordkeeping requirements, https://www.ecfr.gov/current/title-31/subtitle-B/chapter-V/part-501/subpart-C/section-501.601.

42. Baker McKenzie, "OFAC Issues Interim Final Rule Regarding 10-Year Recordkeeping Requirement," October 9, 2024, https://sanctionsnews.bakermckenzie.com/ofac-issues-interim-final-rule-regarding-10-year-recordkeeping-requirement.

43. OFAC, FAQ 12.

44. Department of the Treasury, "Treasury Announces $508 Million Settlement with British American Tobacco Largest Ever Against Non-Financial Institution," April 25, 2023, https://home.treasury.gov/news/press-releases/jy1441.

45. Department of the Treasury, Enforcement Release, "OFAC Settles with Binance Holdings, Ltd for $968,618,825 Related to Apparent Violations of Multiple Sanctions Programs," November 21, 2023, https://ofac.treasury.gov/media/932351/download?inline.

46. Department of Justice, Office of Public Affairs, Press Release, "US Citizen Who Conspired to Assist North Korea in Evading Sanctions Sentenced to Over Five Years and Fined $100,000," April 12, 2022, https://www.justice.gov/opa/pr/us-citizen-who-conspired-assist-north-korea-evading-sanctions-sentenced-over-five-years-and.

47. OFAC, Enforcement Information For August 6, 2015, "Navigators Insurance Company Settles Potential Liability for Apparent Violations of Multiple Sanctions Programs," https://ofac.treasury.gov/media/12361/download?inline.

www.ingramcontent.com/pod-product-compliance
Lightning Source LLC
LaVergne TN
LVHW022312200926
848481LV00004B/1294